Introduction

Teach Children Financial Management - Family Financial Journey

Have you ever worried about how to effectively teach your children about money and personal finance? Do you want to build a prosperous and sustainable future for your family, but you're not sure where to start?

The book "Teach Children Financial Management - Family Financial Journey" will help you overcome the challenges on the path of financial management and create a bright financial future for your children. Authored by [PHAN TUAN], an experienced financial expert and a happy family father, this book promises to provide you with practical knowledge, honest advice, and reliable financial plans.

What you will find in this book:

1. Journeying alongside your children on the financial path: This book not only equips you with financial knowledge but also helps you become a guiding figure for your children, understanding their thoughts, and walking with them step by step on an exciting financial journey.
2. Easy-to-understand and applicable financial knowledge: You don't need to be a financial expert to grasp and apply the knowledge in this book. All concepts are explained clearly and accompanied by real-life examples to make it easy for you to integrate into your daily life.
3. Building an emergency fund and smart investments: The book will guide you in establishing an emergency fund for your family, teach you how to make intelligent investments, and seize effective financial investment opportunities.

4. Family financial management and risk reduction: Learn how to scientifically and efficiently manage your family budget, enabling you to achieve long-term financial goals while minimizing financial risks in life.
5. Financial management in the family and overcoming life events: Confronting significant life events such as marriage, buying a house, having children, or emergency situations, you will acquire the skills to confidently manage your finances and make the most of opportunities and challenges.

"Teach Children Financial Management - Family Financial Journey" will be your reliable companion in constructing a prosperous future for your family. To embark on the financial journey with your children, turn to the first page and discover the invaluable secrets and beneficial advice in this book.

Together, let's build a strong family and attain financial freedom!

Foreword: Family Finance - A Guide to Teaching Children Saving and Successful Investment

Life has taught me that teaching children about money management is not merely about conveying numbers or financial concepts. It is a sincere process that demands patience and a heart filled with love. Along the journey of teaching my children about finance, I have come to realize that there are no secrets, only steadfast steps and genuine knowledge.

This book is born out of my passion for sharing practical financial knowledge and experiences, helping parents and children learn and grow together in money management. I believe that teaching children about financial management is not just about providing short-term solutions but also about building a solid foundation for them to confidently face financial challenges in the future.

"Family Finance - A Guide to Teaching Children Saving and Successful Investment" is not merely a dry instructional guide; it is a heartfelt and intimate sharing from a father's heart. From genuine advice to real-life examples in daily living, my hope is that this book will offer you helpful insights and approaches to finance, enabling you and your children to come closer to your financial goals.

Within the pages of this book, we will learn together about money management, building emergency funds, smart investing, risk reduction, and facing significant life events. I believe that these knowledge and skills will not only apply to financial management but also contribute to building a prosperous, happy, and meaningful life for your family.

Let's embark on this exciting and meaningful financial journey together. I hope this book becomes your reliable companion, guiding you and your children towards financial and life achievements. Alongside our children, we can construct a bright and dream-worthy financial future.

Gratitude Note

We sincerely extend our heartfelt thanks to those who have accompanied us and contributed to the completion of the book "Family Finance - A Guide to Teaching Children Saving and Successful Investment." This book would not have been possible without the support and contributions from those around us. We want to express our deep appreciation and dedication to:

Family and children: Our first words of gratitude go to our family and children - an immense source of motivation for writing this book. Your support, care, and loving presence have been an indescribable source of inspiration.

Financial experts: We extend our gratitude to the financial experts and researchers who have contributed their expertise and invaluable experiences, making this book a reliable source of knowledge.

Readers: Lastly, we want to express sincere thanks to all the readers who have devoted their precious time to read this book. We hope that the book has provided you with valuable knowledge and helped you gain a better understanding of family finance, enabling you to achieve your cherished financial goals.

This book could not exist without the support and contributions from those who helped shape it. We are truly grateful and touched by the genuine emotions shared with us. The book belongs not only to us but to all those who have accompanied us on this journey and contributed to its creation.

Once again, we extend our heartfelt thanks to everyone!

With warm regards,

Chapter 1

Introduction Guiding Children in Financial Management

The path to a fulfilled and stable financial future for children begins with the earliest steps in life. Teaching children how to manage money and understand the value of finances is an immensely crucial task that parents and educators must undertake. This e-book, "Teaching Children Financial Management," is written to familiarize you with effective approaches in teaching children about finances, from the simplest concepts to more complex lessons.

1.1 Why is financial management an important skill?

Finance is the heart of life, and its significant role in every aspect of our lives cannot be denied. However, how do we educate children about finances, helping them build a strong foundation for the future? This is a question that many parents and caregivers are asking.

This book not only focuses on conveying fundamental knowledge about money and finances to children but also guides them on how to apply this knowledge in their everyday lives. From saving money, building income sources to making intelligent investments, together we will explore the steps towards their financial independence.

1.2 Seize the opportunity - Start early

The best time to start teaching children about finances is not later, when they have grown up and stepped into independent life. While learning and challenges will continue throughout their lives, the basic foundation of finance should be built from the early years.

This book will equip you with the necessary knowledge to create a positive financial education environment in your family, school, and daily life of your children. By supporting them from their early years, we will help them develop healthy financial habits and saving awareness while providing them with essential skills to face an ever-changing future.

Let's explore and build a sustainable financial future for our children!

1.3 Book structure

To facilitate your access to and application of knowledge, this book is divided into specific topic chapters. Each chapter focuses on a particular aspect of financial management, providing knowledge, advice, and practical lessons based on experience.

Chapter 2: The Importance of Saving in Life

Chapter 3: Saving for Children - Advice for Parents

Chapter 4: Financial Strategies for Children

Chapter 5: Building a Strong Future

Chapter 6: Developing Financial Mindset for Children

Chapter 7: Mastering Basic Financial Skills

Chapter 8: Cultivating Good Financial Habits

Chapter 9: Creating Long-term Financial Plans

Chapter 10: Building a Sustainable Financial Future

Chapter 11: Crafting Investment Plans

Chapter 12: Finance and Family

Chapter 13: Finance and Married Life

Chapter 14: Investment and Asset Building

Chapter 15: Finance and Retirement

Chapter 16: Debt Management and Financial Strengthening

Chapter 17: Financial Risk Management

Chapter 18: Finance and Family Conclusion: Financial Journey with Children

1.4 Conclusion

The book "Family Finance - A Guide to Teaching Children Successful Saving and Investing" is a journey together to explore and build a solid foundation for the financial lives of our children. By focusing on educating children about finances from an early age, we are sending an important message about independence, decision-making, and responsibility. We hope that this book will be a source of inspiration and a useful tool to help you build a bright financial future for your children.

Let us embark on this journey and dedicate the most meaningful moments to teaching children financial management – something vital not only for today but also for the long-lasting future.

Wishing you success and happiness on the path of teaching children financial management!

1.5 Why Teaching Children Financial Management is Important

In the modern age, finance plays a crucial role not only in personal life but also in the development and prosperity of a nation. However, many adults have had to learn and face significant financial issues without proper guidance or basic knowledge from an early age.

It is essential not to let our children experience the difficulties and consequences of not knowing how to manage finances. Teaching children money management and finance from an early age is not only about imparting knowledge but also about building a healthy attitude and habits towards money.

1.6 Why teaching children financial management is important:

1.6.1 Instill early savings consciousness and financial orientation:

Developing a savings consciousness and financial orientation from an early age helps children understand the value of money and learn how to use it responsibly. By teaching children to save and prioritize their expenses, we support the creation of a healthy financial environment for the future.

1.6.2 Prevent future financial problems:

Teaching children how to manage finances from a young age equips them with the necessary skills and awareness to avoid potential financial problems in the future. They will learn how to avoid uncontrolled debts and how to manage finances efficiently.

1.6.3 Build a foundation for a prosperous future:

Teaching children financial management from an early age provides them with the opportunity to develop and build a prosperous future. Skills in money management and intelligent investments help our children create financial opportunities and ensure a more stable life.

1.6.4 Foster confident and financially independent attitudes:

When children know how to manage finances, they develop a confident and financially independent attitude. From organizing daily expenses to making investment choices and long-term financial plans, the ability to manage finances empowers them to face any situation confidently.

1.7 Accompanying our children on the financial journey

In this book, we will experience a meaningful journey together to build a strong foundation for the financial lives of our children. By accompanying and learning together, we will make solid progress and spark inspiration in our children to understand money, finance, and responsible management.

Let's explore useful financial management skills and secrets, helping our children develop comprehensively and reach a financially bright future!

1.8 Target readers of the book

The book aims to guide and provide useful information for parents, teachers, educators, and anyone interested in helping children understand financial management and building a solid foundation in money matters.

1.8.1 Parents and caregivers

The role of parents and caregivers is the most crucial in teaching children financial management. This book will provide parents with clear and specific guidance on how to impart basic financial knowledge to their children, along with practical lessons and activities to apply in daily life.

1.8.2 Teachers and educators

For teachers and educators, educating children about financial management is an essential part of comprehensive teaching. This book offers helpful suggestions, activities, and resources to integrate financial topics into teaching plans and curricula.

1.8.3 Children and adolescents

Financial management is not only for adults. Children and adolescents can also learn and apply basic money knowledge in their daily lives. This book will provide easily understandable information and fun activities to help children grasp fundamental financial skills.

1.9 Book content and how to use it

The book is divided into specific chapters focusing on important aspects of financial management, from saving and spending to investing and long-term financial planning. Each chapter contains fundamental knowledge and practical lessons, along with understandable examples and activities to apply in real life.

The book is not merely a source of knowledge but also a supportive tool for teaching and discussing with children. Parents, teachers, and educators can use the book to create engaging and relatable lessons for children, helping them understand and become more interested in financial management.

1.10 Ultimately, where will we go?

The book is a powerful educational tool to build a solid foundation in money and financial matters for our children. By supporting children in developing saving habits, understanding the value of money, and learning financial management, we are preparing them for a promising future.

Let us empower our children to confidently face life's challenges with a sustainable financial life. Together, we will create a generation of financially savvy, reliable, and independent individuals.

We embark on this journey together – with trust and hope!

1.11 Continuing the journey

The book is not just a stopping point in this important journey. It is a bridge that opens new doors and continues to inspire further financial discoveries for our children. We will continue to accompany and emphasize the importance of making small daily strides

1.12 Things You Need to Prepare

In this journey, there are some things you need to prepare. First and foremost, be willing to dedicate time and effort to learn about finances together with your children. Create a comfortable and engaging learning environment while welcoming your children's questions and concerns with an open and dedicated heart.

Secondly, prepare yourself to learn alongside your children. Although you may already have experience and knowledge about finances, teaching your children is also an opportunity for you to explore new ideas and look at issues from different perspectives.

Lastly, set clear and realistic goals for teaching children financial management. You don't have to be perfect from the start; what matters is that we take steps together and make efforts to understand and apply financial knowledge to daily life.

1.13 Let's Create a Strong Financial Future Together

The book is not only about teaching children about money but also about creating a solid financial future for our children. As we journey and learn together, we not only provide our children with financial knowledge but also impart essential values and principles for their development and growth.

Together, we will explore worthwhile financial journeys. We will learn from mistakes and challenges while enjoying successes and progress. Let's build a stable financial future where our children can confidently and independently face life and pursue their dreams.

Let's embark on this important journey and let the book "Family Finance - A Guide to Teaching Children Successful Saving and Investing" be the source of inspiration and guidance for the financial lives of our children.

1.14 The Journey Begins - Thank You for Joining

Thank you for choosing the book "Family Finance - A Guide to Teaching Children Successful Saving and Investing" to participate in this meaningful journey. By accompanying and dedicating time to learn about finances with our children, we have made a significant commitment to building a solid financial future for the next generation.

Let's start this journey with patience and dedication. What matters is not how fast we go, but that we go in the right direction, one step at a time. This book will be your reliable companion, supporting and providing the necessary knowledge to effectively teach your children about finances.

Together, let's create a positive and engaging learning environment where our children can understand and apply financial knowledge to their daily lives. Let's discover useful financial secrets and skills together and cherish the meaningful moments when we see our children grow and confidently face the future.

Together, we will build a generation of financially savvy, confident, and independent individuals. The book "Family Finance - A Guide to Teaching Children Successful Saving and Investing" hopes to be an inspiring and valuable support in this important journey.

Chapter 2:

The Importance of Saving in Life

In Chapter 2, we will delve into the importance of saving in life and why teaching children how to save from a young age is a crucial factor in building a strong financial foundation for our children. We will explore the benefits of saving and how to instill this value in children, from small daily activities to significant financial decisions in life.

2.1 Saving - The First and Important Step

Saving is a fundamental and essential concept in our lives. It is not just about spending less money; it also requires understanding the true value of money and the ability to manage finances wisely. When we save, we create opportunities to use money effectively and build a more stable financial life.

2.2 Why Teach Children to Save from an Early Age?

Developing a savings consciousness and healthy financial management habits from a young age will have a significant positive impact on children's lives in the future. By saving from a young age, children will have a better understanding of the value of money and how to use it responsibly. This helps them develop the technical mindset for financial management and form automatic saving habits in their daily lives.

2.3 Starting with Small Steps - Teaching Children to Save from Collecting Bottle Deposits

A great way to begin teaching children about saving is through small daily activities. For example, teaching children to save money from collecting bottle deposits, small gift boxes, or daily pocket money. Such activities not only help children understand the value of money but also cultivate patience and perseverance in saving.

2.4 Building a "Savings Jar" and Tracking Children's Saving Progress

An effective way for children to learn about saving is to build their own "savings jar." The savings jar could be a physical container for real money or a virtual savings account on a phone. By tracking and managing the saved money in the jar, children will have the opportunity to see their progress and feel enthusiastic about the saving process.

2.5 Encouraging Creativity and Exploration in Saving Money

Saving money doesn't necessarily mean cutting back and restricting. We can encourage children to express creativity and exploration in saving money. For example, teaching children to make toys from recycled materials, engaging in free activities, or taking advantage of discounts and offers to save on expenses.

2.6 The Benefits of Saving

In this chapter, we will summarize the valuable benefits that saving brings to children and the entire family. From creating peace of mind in financial matters to the ability to build a strong future, saving is an essential skill that helps children develop and succeed in life.

Saving is not just about accumulating money each month; it brings many significant benefits to our lives and our children's future. Here are the worthy benefits that saving provides:

2.6.1 Creating Peace of Mind and Financial Stability

When we save, we create a financial reserve that helps us feel at ease and confident in facing unforeseen difficulties or situations. During emergencies, we can use the saved money to resolve issues easily and avoid financial worries.

2.6.2 Developing Healthy Financial Management Habits

Saving helps children develop healthy financial management habits from a young age. By saving a portion of their income, children understand the value of hard work and learn to use money responsibly. This habit will stay with them throughout their lives and help them become smart and confident financial managers.

2.6.3 Building a Strong Financial Foundation for the Future

Saving from a young age helps children build a solid financial foundation for the future. Whether it's fulfilling personal dreams and goals, traveling, studying, or purchasing significant assets, saving provides them with the financial resources to confidently pursue these aspirations without having to borrow or fall into debt.

2.6.4 Learning to Prioritize and Assess True Value of Items

Saving helps children learn to prioritize and assess the true value of an item before making a purchase. Instead of spending money on unnecessary things, they tend to make smart shopping choices and focus on what truly matters and has long-term value.

2.6.5 Developing Patience and Perseverance

Saving is a process that requires patience and perseverance. Children need to learn to save money gradually with a plan and avoid impulsive spending. This patience and perseverance help them control their emotions and face life's challenges.

2.6.6 Discovering Joy in Saving

Saving is not about deprivation and restrictions. Children can discover joy in saving money smartly and efficiently. For example, saving money to buy a long-desired item or to fulfill a dream vacation will bring excitement and pride in themselves.

2.7 Take the Time and Dedication to Teach Children About Saving

Teaching Children about saving is not just about imparting knowledge; it is also a process of interaction and dedication from parents. Take the time to talk to your children about the value of money, how to save, and the benefits it brings. When we dedicate ourselves to teaching children about saving, we are investing in their future.

2.7.1 Create a Comfortable and Positive Learning Environment

To help children learn and apply the knowledge of saving, we need to create a comfortable and positive learning environment. Encourage your children to ask questions, express opinions, and share thoughts about saving and financial management. By listening to and respecting their perspectives, we can create a nurturing space for development and growth.

2.7.2 Establish Personal Savings Jars

Encourage your children to establish personal savings jars. Each family member can have their own savings jar, where they record the amount saved each week or month. This helps children recognize their increasing savings and feel a sense of progress in their saving journey.

2.7.3 Encourage Participation in Saving Activities

Encourage your children to participate in meaningful saving activities. This could involve using natural light instead of electricity during the day, turning off water when not in use, or using reusable bags instead of plastic bags when shopping. Such small actions help children better understand the importance of saving in their daily lives.

2.7.4 Set Saving Goals and Explore Ways to Improve Savings

Teach your children how to set saving goals and improve their saving habits. You can guide them to set savings goals for an item they want to own or to save a certain amount of money within a specific time frame. When they achieve their goals, encourage and praise them to motivate continued saving in the future.

2.7.5 Teach Children to Evaluate the True Value of Items Before Shopping

When shopping with your children, teach them to evaluate the true value of an item before making a purchase. Encourage them to think about the necessity and long-term usefulness of the item, whether it genuinely meets their needs. This way, we help children develop smart shopping skills and financial independence in spending money.

2.8 Saving is a Lifelong Journey

The journey of saving is not a short-term task; it is a lifelong process. Together, we learn, experience, and improve every day to build a strong financial future for our children. Teaching children about saving not only helps them have a financially stable life but also serves as a significant investment for their maturity and success in the future.

2.8.1 Saving is a Smart Balance Between Consumption and Accumulation

In modern life, consumption and saving often become a balancing act. We want to enjoy life and fulfill personal needs, but at the same time, we also want to save to ensure a stable future. Finding a smart balance between consumption and accumulation is crucial in managing family finances and teaching children to do the same from a young age.

2.8.2 Learn from Successful Role Models

We can learn from successful role models in financial management. Stories of people who have succeeded in saving and achieving financial goals will inspire and motivate our children. We can also share stories of financial mistakes and learn from those experiences to help children avoid similar mistakes.

2.8.3 Focus on Continuous Financial Education

Financial education is an ongoing and never-ending process. Keep the conversation and learning about finances open and regular. Read books, watch educational videos about finances, or participate in financial courses designed for children. By investing time and effort in continuous financial education, we help our children build knowledge and awareness of money from a young age.

2.9 Savings Milestones - When to Save?

Teaching children about savings milestones is essential to help them understand how to manage money in their daily lives. Guide your children about important savings milestones, such as:

2.9.1 Daily Spending Savings

Encourage your children to save money on daily expenses such as candies, toys, or fast food. This helps them understand the importance of distinguishing between necessary and unnecessary expenses and focus on saving for more significant goals.

2.9.2 Savings for Festivals, Holidays, and Special Occasions

Teach your children to save money for festivals, holidays, and special occasions as a great way to learn how to manage expenses and prepare financially for these events. Spend time with them to plan and track their savings progress for each occasion.

2.9.3 Savings for Shopping and Big Purchases

When they want to buy a big-ticket item, teach your children how to save money for that goal. You can help them create a step-by-step savings plan and set a specific timeframe to achieve it. This helps children understand the saving process and see themselves contributing to achieving their dreams.

2.9.4 Savings for Education and the Future

Encourage your children to save money for education and the future. This could be for studying abroad, pursuing higher education, or investing in personal skill-enhancing courses. By saving for education, children will realize the importance and value of investing in themselves.

2.9.5 Savings for Retirement

Teach your children about saving money for retirement to instill a long-term financial planning mindset. Explain to them the benefits of saving for retirement early in life, enabling them to be financially independent and not reliant on others in their old age.

2.9.6 Savings for Emergencies

Not only saving for big goals but also teach your children to save money for emergencies. Explain to them the importance of having an emergency fund to deal with unexpected difficulties like job loss, illnesses, or natural disasters.

2.10 Guiding Children in Setting Saving Goals and Improving Savings

2.10.1 Listen to and Understand Children's Desires

To guide children in setting saving goals, we need to listen to and understand their desires. Discuss with them what they want to save for and why. We can suggest suitable saving ideas based on their age and vision, but let them actively participate in goal-setting and choosing how to save.

2.10.2 Establish Specific and Clear Goals

Once we understand their desires, help them set specific and clear saving goals. Ensure that the goals are reasonable and significant for them, such as saving enough to buy a favorite item, saving for extracurricular activities, or saving a portion of money for home decoration.

2.10.3 Plan and Track Saving Progress

After setting the saving goals, assist your children in planning specific timeframes and steps to achieve those goals. Discuss with them how much money to save each week or month and how to execute that saving plan. Additionally, track their saving progress together, so they can see their advancements and achievements according to the plan.

2.10.4 Encourage and Praise Saving Achievements

Encouragement and praise play essential roles in supporting children to reach their saving goals. Motivate and support them throughout the saving process, through reminders and respect for their efforts. When children achieve their saving goals, praise them and help them recognize the value of patience and perseverance in their saving journey.

2.11 Cultivating Sustainable Saving Habits

2.11.1 Saving is a Habit, Not an Event

Emphasize that saving is not merely a one-time event or action; it is a sustainable lifestyle habit. To become savers, we need to practice saving daily and maintain this habit over time. Encourage children to understand that saving is an integral part of life and should be nurtured and developed as a sustainable habit.

2.11.2 Utilizing Saving Opportunities

Teach your children to seize saving opportunities in their daily lives. One classic example is taking advantage of discounts, promotions, or offers to shop more economically. We can also make use of free activities, such as participating in public events, going for walks, or enjoying nature, to save on entertainment costs.

2.11.3 Facing Challenges in the Saving Process

During the saving process, challenges and temptations may arise, making it easy for us to fall into unnecessary spending. Teach your children how to confront these challenges and control their emotions. Help them realize the importance of patience and avoiding impulsive spending, so they can achieve sustainable saving goals.

2.11.4 Cultivating and Sustaining a Positive Saving Habit

Lastly, actively cultivate and maintain a saving habit in your children's daily lives. Encourage them to save a portion of their monthly income while finding ways to save and grow their wealth through smart investments and effective financial management.

2.11.5 Focusing on Long-term Values

Guide your children to focus on the long-term values of saving rather than short-term benefits. This can involve fulfilling dreams and future goals or building a strong financial foundation. Help them contemplate the genuine significance and meaning of saving in life.

2.11.6 Supporting and Participating Together

To develop saving habits in your children, support and engage with them. Be a role model by practicing responsible saving and financial management yourself. Simultaneously, participate in the saving process together with your children through discussions, planning, and monitoring their saving progress.

2.11.7 Creating Opportunities to Earn Extra Money

Encourage your children to find ways to earn extra money by taking on small jobs or engaging in age-appropriate money-making activities. Earning extra money not only helps them save more but also teaches them the value of hard work and money.

2.11.8 Not Evaluating Failure by the Amount Saved

In the saving journey, there may be times when your children can't achieve their initial saving goals. Teach them not to measure failure solely by the amount saved but rather by the effort they put in and the lessons they learn from the process. Encourage them not to be discouraged but to persevere and work towards their saving goals in the future.

2.12 Saving is a Joyful and Worthy Journey

Above all, remind your children that saving is a joyful and worthwhile journey. It not only helps them build a strong financial future but also develops essential skills such as patience, financial management, and understanding true value in life.

Teaching your children about saving is not just about imparting knowledge; it is an investment in their future. Let's learn, experience, and improve together in this saving journey. By teaching them saving from an early age, we are helping them become smart and confident financial managers, ready to face any challenges that life presents.

2.12.1 Learning through Reading and Exploring Financial Knowledge

Encourage your children to read books about saving and finance. Children's books on saving not only provide valuable knowledge but also make financial concepts easy for them to understand. Additionally, explore online resources and educational videos about finance with your children.

2.12.2 Creating Saving-related Games and Activities

Design saving-related games and activities to engage your children. For instance, you could create a spinning wheel game with different saving goals, and each time your children save the corresponding amount, they get to spin the wheel and receive a small reward. Alternatively, organize a drawing contest about saving, allowing your children to express their ideas and thoughts about money.

2.12.3 Setting Financial Goals and Planning to Achieve Them

Encourage your children to set financial goals and help them plan to achieve those dreams. These goals could be purchasing a special item they desire, traveling to a destination they want to explore, or investing in a favorite extracurricular activity. Support them in identifying the amount they need to save and creating a step-by-step plan to realize their aspirations.

2.12.4 Leveraging Financial Tools for Children

Today, there are various financial tools designed for children to manage money easily and enjoyably. Take advantage of savings apps, electronic wallets, or dedicated savings accounts for children to help them track and manage their savings. These tools can also provide age-appropriate financial information and guidance tailored to their needs.

2.12.5 Creating a Space for Financial Discussions within the Family

Create a positive and regular space within the family to discuss finances and saving. These conversations should not only focus on saving money but also serve as an opportunity for your children to learn from the experiences and advice of their parents. Foster an open and sincere environment for your children to feel comfortable sharing their thoughts and questions about money.

2.13 Above All, Love and Care

Lastly, remember that teaching your children about saving and financial management requires love, care, and patience. Throughout this process, you may encounter challenges and difficulties, but what matters is that you never give up and always support your children.

Show your love and care as parents throughout your children's saving and financial management journey. Here are some ways to demonstrate that love and care:

2.13.1 Lead by Example, Not Just Instruction

In addition to imparting knowledge about saving and finance, be a living example for your children. Show them through your actions that saving is an essential part of daily life. When your children witness you saving and managing finances responsibly, they will naturally learn and apply those principles in their own lives.

2.13.2 Create a Positive Environment and Encourage Your Children

Create a positive environment and encourage your children in their saving and financial management endeavors. Support and motivate them in every step, regardless of the ultimate outcome. Focus not only on the results but also respect the process and their efforts. When they see that you are there for them, believing in their capabilities, they will feel confident and enthusiastic about saving.

2.13.3 Assist Your Children in Crafting Saving Plans and Monitoring Progress

Support your children in devising specific saving plans and timelines to achieve their goals. Collaborate with them in planning, helping them gain a clearer understanding of what it takes to fulfill their dreams. Simultaneously, track their saving progress together, allowing them to experience their own growth and accomplishments.

2.13.4 Respect and Listen to Your Children's Thoughts

Respect and listen to your children's thoughts about money and saving. Encourage them to freely and sincerely share their opinions and ideas. When parents listen and respect their children's viewpoints, they feel valued and treated fairly, leading them to engage more actively in the saving process.

2.13.5 Confront Mistakes and Support Learning from Them

In the saving journey, your children may make mistakes or lose patience. Teach them to face these mistakes with maturity and support them in learning from those experiences. Mistakes are a natural part of learning, and we can gain valuable insights from them. Encourage your children not to get discouraged but to keep striving and improving to achieve their saving goals.

2.14 Striking a Balance Between Saving and Enjoying Life

Lastly, help your children strike a balance between saving and enjoying life. Saving does not mean deprivation and observing everything pass by. Encourage your children to savor life responsibly and mindfully. Together, prioritize what truly matters and is worth spending money and time on for more significant financial experiences and goals.

2.15 Conclusion

Teaching children about saving and financial management is not just about imparting knowledge; it is an investment in their future. By teaching children to save from an early age, we help them develop essential skills and confidence to face life's challenges.

This book has introduced the importance of saving, the benefits of teaching children to save from a young age, and ways to guide children in setting saving goals and building sustainable saving habits. Furthermore, we have explored methods to encourage and support children throughout their saving journey, as well as achieving a balance between saving and enjoying life.

When we care for and support children in their saving journey, we are showing them love and concern for their future. Teaching children to save is a significant task that requires patience, companionship, and attentive listening. However, it is a worthwhile endeavor that brings immense benefits to all of us.

I hope this book has provided you with knowledge, advice, and inspiration to continue supporting and educating children about saving and financial management. Let's work together to build a solid and sustainable financial future for our children, so they can confidently and successfully navigate through life.

Chapter 3

Saving for Children - Tips for Parents

3.1 Financial Education for Children: The Important Role of Parents

In this chapter, we will focus on the crucial role of parents in providing financial education to their children. Parents play a guiding role, imparting knowledge, and creating conditions for children to develop saving habits and financial management from a young age.

3.2 Identifying Saving and Financial Goals for Children

Before teaching children to save, we need to identify saving and financial goals for them. This helps parents and children have shared goals and direction in the process of saving and financial management.

3.3 Effective Ways to Convey Financial Knowledge to Children

In this section, we will explore effective ways to convey financial knowledge to children that are suitable for their age and mentality.

3.4 Creating a Positive Environment and Encouraging Saving

To help children develop saving habits, we need to create a positive and encouraging environment within the family. Let's explore practical ways to achieve this.

3.5 Managing Finances in the Family and Setting an Example for Children

Managing finances in the family plays a crucial role in teaching children about saving and financial matters. Let's learn how to set an example for children through the actions of the family.

3.6 Understanding and Using Financial Tools for Children

Lastly, we will explore financial tools designed specifically for children and how to use them to support children in saving and financial management.

3.6.1 Savings Account for Children

A savings account is a common and secure financial tool for children. Parents can help children open a savings account at a bank or a reputable financial institution. A savings account helps children develop saving habits and provides a safe and small return on their money.

3.6.2 E-wallets for Children

Today, there are numerous e-wallet applications designed specifically for children. Parents can assist children in creating an e-wallet account and managing their savings through this app. E-wallets not only help children easily track their savings but also provide learning opportunities and incentives through engaging features.

3.6.3 Financial Educational Games and Apps

There are many financial educational games and apps specifically designed for children. These games help children learn about money and finance in an exciting and interactive way. Parents can download and play these games with their children to encourage and support their financial learning.

3.6.4 Learning from Real-Life Experiences

Encourage children to participate in real-life experiences involving money and finances. For example, allow them to be part of the shopping process to better understand the value of money and budget management. Additionally, encourage children to set aside a portion of their income for saving or investing in financial goals.

3.6.5 Supporting and Listening to Children

While supporting children in saving and financial management, parents need to listen to their opinions and thoughts. Encourage children to share what they have learned and the challenges they are facing. Provide support and encouragement to help them overcome obstacles and continue developing saving habits and financial management.

3.7 Creating Conditions for Learning and Experiencing

Lastly, create conditions for children to learn and experience money and finance. Explore the financial world with them through reading books, watching educational videos, attending classes, or even learning from financial educators.

3.8 Building Financial Skills for Children

Building financial skills for children is a significant process that helps them develop smart money management abilities. In this chapter, we will explore how to help children develop the necessary financial skills to become confident and responsible financial managers.

3.8.1 Distinguishing "Wants" and "Needs"

Help children understand the difference between what they "want" and what they "need." This helps them learn to prioritize and spend wisely. Teach children that not everything they desire is essential and that saving and spending on what truly matters is crucial.

3.8.2 Understanding Budgets and Money

Introduce children to the concept of budgets and help them understand how to manage money effectively. Assist children in creating budgets for daily activities, education, entertainment, and saving. This helps them grasp the amount of money they have and how to allocate and use it responsibly.

3.8.3 Basic Financial Skills

Help children develop basic financial skills such as calculating, counting money, understanding different currencies, and how to use them. This makes them more confident and capable in managing their daily finances.

3.8.4 Creating Opportunities for Children to Earn Money

Create opportunities for children to earn money by engaging in extracurricular activities, neighborhood services, or small jobs. Earning money not only helps children become more independent but also provides them with a chance to learn about the value of hard work and money.

3.9 Developing Sustainable Saving and Financial Management Habits

3.9.1 Creating Long-term Saving Plans

Support children in creating long-term saving plans by helping them set specific saving goals and determining the amount of money needed to achieve those goals. Encourage them to regularly assess their progress and make adjustments to the saving plan if necessary.

3.9.2 Promoting Saving Habits in Daily Life

Encourage children to practice saving in their daily lives. For example, turning off lights when not in use, avoiding food wastage, using water and energy efficiently, and making smart shopping choices to save costs.

3.9.3 Learning to Resist Temptations of Excessive Spending

As children develop saving and financial management habits, they will face temptations of excessive spending. Help them recognize these temptations and learn how to confront them with mindfulness and patience. Additionally, support them in finding alternative forms of entertainment and enjoyment rather than relying on unnecessary spending.

3.10 Evaluating and Monitoring Progress

Finally, evaluate and monitor the progress of children in their saving and financial management journey. Listen to their stories and experiences and assess the positive changes that saving habits bring to their lives. This helps children understand the value of saving and feel proud of the steps they have taken.

3.11 Conclusion

In this chapter, we have learned about building financial skills for children, including distinguishing "wants" and "needs," understanding budgets and money, and developing basic financial skills such as calculations, counting money, and using currencies.

We have seen the importance of creating opportunities for children to earn money and promoting saving habits in their daily lives. Additionally, we have supported them in learning to resist temptations of excessive spending and provided opportunities for them to learn and experience money and finance.

Through building financial skills for children, we help them develop smart and confident money management abilities. This makes them more independent and prepared to face financial challenges in life.

Chapter 4

Financial Strategies for Children

4.1 Building a Savings Fund for Children

One of the essential financial strategies for children is building a savings fund. In this chapter, we will explore how to build a savings fund for children and the benefits of doing so.

4.1.1 Choosing Suitable Savings Options

Learn about suitable savings options for children, such as savings accounts, investment funds, or e-wallet accounts designed specifically for children. Consider factors such as interest rates, risks, and convenience to select the most appropriate savings option.

4.1.2 Setting Saving Goals

Help children identify specific saving goals, such as buying their favorite toys, saving for vacations, or contributing to an educational fund. Clear saving goals provide motivation and direction for children in their saving and financial management journey.

4.1.3 Regular Savings

Encourage children to save regularly by setting aside a small portion of their rewards, lucky money, or earnings from part-time jobs. Regular saving helps children develop saving habits and accumulate money steadily and sustainably.

4.1.4 Providing Support and Monitoring Progress

Support children throughout their saving journey and monitor their progress. This helps them feel cared for and trusted, while also allowing parents to track and assist them in successfully achieving their saving goals.

4.2 Investment and Financial Risk Education

If children have accumulated enough savings, parents can guide and educate them about investment and financial risk. Teach children about different types of investments such as stocks, bonds, investment funds, or real estate. However, it is important to note that investing involves risk and should be approached carefully and prudently.

4.2.1 Understanding Investments

Introduce children to the basics of investment, from different investment opportunities to calculating returns and risks. Encourage them to research information from reliable sources and make investment decisions based on accurate information and analysis.

4.2.2 Grasping Financial Risks

During investment education, help children understand financial risks and how to confront them thoughtfully. Explain to them that investments can bring high profits but can also face failure. It is crucial for them to comprehend and evaluate risks before making investment decisions.

4.2.3 Virtual Investment Practice

Before actually investing real money, encourage children to practice virtual investments through online investment simulation games. This helps them practice investment skills, learn about financial markets, and face risks in a safe environment. Practicing virtual investment boosts their confidence when they step into the real investment market.

4.2.4 Adjusting Investment Strategies

Encourage children to understand that investment is an ongoing process and requires adapting and adjusting investment strategies according to market conditions and personal financial situations. Teach them how to reassess and adjust their investment strategies when necessary to ensure their investments remain safe and effective.

4.3 Building Smart Saving Habits in Daily Life

In addition to saving money, we can also build smart saving habits in daily life to help children learn how to use resources efficiently and sustainably.

4.3.1 Saving Energy and Water

Guide children on how to use energy and water efficiently. Encourage them to turn off electronic devices when not in use, switch off lights when leaving a room, and use water sparingly in daily activities. These habits not only save costs but also protect the environment.

4.3.2 Smart Shopping

Teach children how to shop smartly by comparing prices, seeking deals and discounts, and purchasing only what they truly need. Encourage them to think carefully before making purchases and question themselves if the items they are buying are genuinely necessary.

4.3.3 Understanding Borrowing and Lending

If children are of appropriate age, explain borrowing and lending to them. Help them understand interest rates, terms, and commitments when borrowing money. At the same time, encourage them to avoid unnecessary borrowing and set saving goals to avoid endless debts.

4.3.4 Exploring Different Saving Methods

Finally, explore and experiment with different saving methods with children. It could be reusing items instead of buying new ones, utilizing deals and discounts, or even making some basic products themselves. Encourage children to find saving methods that suit them and become smart savers in their daily lives.

4.4 Continuous Financial Education

The process of financial education for children is not a one-time event but an ongoing journey throughout their lives. Ensure that children continue to learn and experience financial matters, while providing support and encouragement when they face financial challenges in the future.

4.4.1 Creating Opportunities for Financial Learning

Create opportunities for children to learn about finances through reading books, watching educational videos, attending classes, or even learning from financial experts. This helps them stay updated on financial knowledge and gain a better understanding of the financial market and new investment opportunities.

4.4.2 Providing Support in Facing Financial Challenges

Throughout their lives, children will encounter various financial challenges. Always be willing to support them in resolving complex financial issues and help them confidently handle difficult situations. Be a reliable companion and encourage them to overcome all difficulties.

4.4.3 Encouraging Children to Set Financial Goals

Encourage children to set specific financial goals and strive to achieve them. Help them plan and take systematic and effective actions to reach their goals. Clear financial goals give children motivation and direction in life.

4.4.4 Continuously Learning About Finances

Life constantly changes, and financial rules may also change over time. Encourage children to never stop learning about finances and keep updating their knowledge. Continual learning helps children make smart and effective financial decisions in a complex and changing financial environment.

4.5 Being a Financial Role Model

One of the most important factors in financial education for children is the actions and attitudes of parents. Be a financial role model for children by demonstrating smart saving habits and intelligent financial management in daily life.

4.5.1 Managing Finances Wisely

Manage finances wisely and have a specific plan for saving, investing, and using money. Avoid unnecessary spending actions and always keep an emergency fund for unforeseen situations.

4.5.2 Discussing Money with Children

Engage in discussions with children about money and explain the family's financial decisions. Explain the family budget, the reasons for managing finances in a certain way, and how to practice saving and investing.

4.5.3 Teaching Financial Risk Management

Teach children how to confront financial risks and handle difficult financial situations confidently. Instill patience and determination in dealing with financial issues, while supporting them in seeking appropriate solutions and choices to overcome challenges.

4.5.4 Discussing Emotions and Money

Have discussions with children about emotions and money, especially feelings of worry or anxiety related to financial issues. Help them understand that emotions are a natural part of life and that discussing and seeking support from family and loved ones is the best way to overcome difficulties.

4.6 Building Confidence and Financial Responsibility

Lastly, help children build confidence and financial responsibility. This requires agreement and support from parents and the family. When children are confident and responsible with money, they will be more confident in managing their personal finances and making smart financial decisions in the future.

4.6.1 Encouraging Children to Make Financial Decisions

Encourage children to make financial decisions and allow them to take responsibility for those decisions. This helps them develop confidence and be willing to face the consequences of their decisions.

4.6.2 Supporting and Encouraging Children in Times of Difficulty

During the learning and practice of financial matters, children may face challenges and failures. Always be ready to support and encourage them when they encounter difficulties and encourage them not to give up. This helps them become more confident and willing to face financial challenges in the future.

4.6.3 Allowing Children to Make Choices and Learn from Mistakes

Allow children to make choices and learn from mistakes in managing their finances. This helps them develop skills in self-management and discover more effective ways of saving and investing for the future.

4.6.4 Creating an Environment that Promotes Financial Independence

Lastly, create an environment that promotes financial independence for children. Encourage them to set their own saving and investment goals and support them in achieving these goals independently.

4.7 Business and Entrepreneurial Thinking for Children

In this chapter, we will explore ways to help children understand business and entrepreneurial thinking from an early age. This is an important part of financial education, as it helps children develop creative thinking, leadership skills, and an entrepreneurial spirit.

4.7.1 Exploring the Business World

Introduce children to the business world through simulation games, educational books, or videos. Present different industries and business fields, from small businesses to large companies. Encourage them to learn about famous entrepreneurs and how they succeeded in their business ventures.

4.7.2 Experiencing Entrepreneurship from an Early Age

Encourage children to participate in entrepreneurial activities from an early age. It could be selling homemade products or organizing small business activities such as car washes or street sales. This helps them develop management, communication, and business skills from a young age.

4.7.3 Teaching Business Thinking

Teach children to think about business and creativity in creating value from ideas and services. Encourage them to think beyond limits and find ways to innovate and improve. Business thinking helps children recognize potential opportunities and create value in life and work.

4.7.4 Building Leadership Skills

Encourage children to engage in leadership activities, such as being a team leader in class or participating in clubs and organizations. Building leadership skills helps children learn decision-making, managing others, and guiding peers. These skills are the foundation for entrepreneurship and future career success.

4.8 Creating Entrepreneurship Opportunities for Children

Support children in creating entrepreneurship opportunities and realizing their business ideas. This helps them develop confidence and readiness to seize opportunities in the business world.

4.8.1 Supporting Children's Business Ideas

Always listen to and support children's business ideas. Encourage them to present their ideas and help them analyze and develop those ideas. Do not dismiss their ideas just because they might seem unrealistic. Instead, encourage them to find ways to improve and turn their ideas into reality.

4.8.2 Creating Favorable Conditions for Children's Entrepreneurship

Create favorable conditions for children's entrepreneurship by providing initial capital and resource support. This can be financial support from the family, helping them prepare loan applications, or creating a suitable environment for them to develop their business ideas.

4.8.3 Encouraging Learning from Failures

If children experience failure in their entrepreneurial endeavors, encourage them to learn from mistakes and face challenges with patience. Failure is not a bad thing; it's an opportunity for them to develop skills and continue growing.

4.9 Navigating the Future in the Business Field

Finally, help children navigate their future in the business field if they are interested and passionate about it. This may involve attending college or specialized business courses, participating in internships, and exploring various career opportunities in the business field they are interested in.

4.9.1 Exploring Suitable Business Fields

Encourage your children to learn about different business fields and help them identify areas that align with their passions and interests. They may be interested in finance, marketing, information technology, creative industries, and more. Experience and explore these fields together to provide them with a clear understanding and make informed decisions.

4.9.2 Learning from Successful Entrepreneurs in the Business Field

Encourage your children to learn from successful entrepreneurs in the business field they are interested in. They can read books about accomplished business figures, attend sharing sessions, or seek mentors and guides. Learning from experienced individuals helps children glean valuable lessons and apply them to their own lives and careers.

4.9.3 Building Necessary Skills in the Business Field

Assist your children in building the necessary skills to thrive in their chosen business field. This may include management skills, communication skills, marketing skills, sales skills, analytical and market evaluation skills, and more. Encourage them to participate in activities and courses to hone and develop these skills.

4.10 Inspiring and Encouraging Your Children

Lastly, inspire and encourage your children every day in life and financial learning, investment, and business pursuits. Be a source of motivation and steadfast support when they face challenges and opportunities in the future.

4.10.1 Listening and Accompanying Your Children

Take the time to listen and share with your children about their financial, investment, and business plans and goals. Accompany them throughout their learning and practice, and provide support when they need it.

4.10.2 Encouraging and Commending Your Children's Achievements

Always encourage and commend your children's achievements, no matter how small or grand they may be. This helps them feel valued and motivated to continue growing and improving themselves.

4.10.3 Allowing Space for Self-Expression and Creativity

Create a space for your children to express their ideas and creativity about finance and business. Avoid evaluating and criticizing their ideas from the start, but instead encourage them to confidently present and develop their ideas.

4.10.4 Believing in Your Children's Potential

Above all, believe in your children's potential and encourage them to have confidence in themselves. Convey to them that they can succeed in finance and business if they persevere, learn, and patiently face challenges.

4.11 Conclusion of the Chapter

This chapter has presented ways to help children develop business thinking and entrepreneurship from a young age. We explored the importance of equipping children with financial management knowledge and skills from an early stage. We learned how to teach them about saving, investing, and cultivating positive financial habits. Additionally, the chapter discussed fostering business thinking and entrepreneurship, building social awareness, and creating positive impacts on society and the community.

Through the knowledge and skills instilled from a young age, children will have the opportunity to develop comprehensively and confidently face life and business challenges in the future. They will become financially conscious individuals, adept at managing money effectively and capable of shaping their financial future.

By guiding and accompanying children throughout their learning and development, parents play a crucial role in building a solid financial foundation for their children. This chapter provided suggestions and methods for parents to impart financial knowledge and foster business thinking in an engaging and effective manner.

By helping children develop business thinking, parents not only assist them in achieving financial success but also nurture important character traits such as patience, creativity, responsibility, and perseverance. These qualities will accompany children throughout their lives and enable them to face all challenges and opportunities in life.

4.12 Instruction for Discussions and Activities

Finally, to enhance the effectiveness of imparting financial knowledge and fostering business thinking for your children, here are some activities and discussion questions that parents can apply:

Activity 1: Family Budget Planning

Encourage your children to participate in the process of family budget planning. Together, identify monthly expenses, set short-term and long-term financial goals, and build a savings plan.

Activity 2: Visit Stores and Markets

Take your children to various stores and markets to observe firsthand buying and selling transactions, price negotiations, and gain an understanding of real-world business operations.

Activity 3: Entrepreneurial Planning

Encourage your children to propose their own entrepreneurial ideas. Ask them about the type of business they want to start, the benefits it would bring to the community and customers, and the plan to execute that idea.

Discussion Questions:

What have you learned from this chapter? Share the strengths and weaknesses of your children regarding finance and business.

How do you feel when discussing money and financial plans with your children?

Have you noticed any changes in your children after guiding them on financial and business matters?

What plans do you have to continue helping your children develop business thinking and explore the financial world?

Do you feel more confident in supporting your children in financial management and developing business skills after this chapter?

These activities and discussion questions help parents and children engage in meaningful conversations and interactions, fostering an environment conducive to continuous learning and development for the children.

4.13 Instruction for Practice and Exercises

To reinforce financial and business knowledge for your children, apply the following practice activities and exercises:

Exercise 1: Personal Budget Building

Ask your children to create a personal budget for themselves. They should identify their monthly income (if any) and expenses. Encourage them to find ways to save and invest a portion of their income for long-term benefits.

Exercise 2: Organize a Charity Event

Guide your children in organizing a charity event or fundraising activity for a social cause they care about. They should plan, find partners, and develop promotional strategies to attract community interest and contributions.

Exercise 3: Analyze a Successful Business

Require your children to research and analyze a successful business they admire. They should learn about how the business achieved success, their business strategy, financial management, and positive contributions to society.

Exercise 4: Build a Business Plan

Encourage your children to create a business plan for their entrepreneurial idea. They should identify business goals, potential markets, competitors, marketing strategies, and financial plans.

Exercise 5: Create a Product or Service

Guide your children to create a small product or service and sell it to family and friends. This experience will help them understand the production and marketing process and gain real-life business exposure.

4.14 References

To continue improving knowledge and skills in teaching children financial management and developing business thinking, below are some useful reference materials that parents can explore further:

"Rich Dad Poor Dad" - Author: Robert T. Kiyosaki This book helps reshape perspectives on money and investment, fostering financial awareness and entrepreneurship in children.

"The Millionaire Next Door" - Authors: Thomas J. Stanley, William D. Danko This book analyzes and studies the lifestyle of true millionaires, helping children gain a better understanding of effective financial management.

"Start with Why: How Great Leaders Inspire Everyone to Take Action" - Author: Simon Sinek This book explains how a business's or individual's mission and purpose can create a positive impact on society and customers.

"Lean In: Women, Work, and the Will to Lead" - Author: Sheryl Sandberg Specifically for parents with daughters, this book presents the rights and opportunities for women to engage in business and leadership roles.

"The $100 Startup: Reinvent the Way You Make a Living, Do What You Love, and Create a New Future" - Author: Chris Guillebeau This book offers new approaches to entrepreneurship with minimal capital, guiding children on how to promote their business ideas.

Chapter 5

Building a Solid Future

5.1 Charting the Course for the Future

After learning and applying crucial knowledge on financial management and developing business thinking, Chapter 5 focuses on building a solid future for your children. We will discuss how to help them set goals and directions in life, enabling them to achieve significant and exciting accomplishments.

5.2 Developing a Leadership Mindset

Leadership thinking is essential in helping children become individuals who can lead and influence their surroundings. We will explore the necessary qualities to develop a leadership mindset and how to apply them in daily life.

5.3 Building Communication Skills

Effective communication is crucial for children to convey opinions, information, and ideas clearly and efficiently. We will learn how to build communication skills and apply them in various everyday situations, from meetings to personal discussions.

5.4 Time Management and Prioritizing Tasks

Time management and prioritizing tasks are crucial factors determining effectiveness and success in life. We will learn how to help children build these skills to optimize their time usage and achieve set goals.

5.5 Nurturing Creative Thinking

Creative thinking is the ability to generate innovative solutions and breakthroughs in life. We will explore ways to encourage children to develop creative thinking and discover new opportunities in their careers and lives.

5.6 Making Education and Career Decisions

Career choices are essential aspects of life, and we will discuss how to support children in making decisions about education and career paths that align with their passions and abilities.

5.7 Learning from Failures and Facing Challenges

Failures and challenges are inevitable parts of life. We will explore how to help children learn from these experiences and continuously confront new challenges.

5.8 Building Relationships and Respecting Others

Building relationships and respecting others are fundamental elements in helping children form connections and gain support from those around them. We will discuss how to help children build positive relationships and respect others.

5.9 Creating a Sustainable Future

Lastly, we will focus on helping children create a sustainable future for themselves and their communities. Encourage children to contribute to society and care for the environment to participate in the development and prosperity of the future.

5.10 Setting Goals and Directions

To build a solid future, children need to clearly define their goals and directions. Encourage them to set specific and achievable goals, both short-term and long-term. When children know their direction and goals, it becomes easier for them to make decisions and choices in life.

5.11 Developing Leadership Mindset

Leadership thinking is an essential skill that helps children become leaders and have influence within their community. Encourage them to develop a leadership mindset by taking on responsibilities, helping others, and creating a positive environment around them.

5.12 Building Communication Skills

Communication skills are crucial for effectively expressing opinions and interacting with others. Teach them how to listen and understand others, express their ideas clearly, and respect different viewpoints. Communication skills will help children build good relationships and achieve success in all aspects of life.

5.13 Time Management and Prioritizing Tasks

The ability to manage time and prioritize tasks is a decisive factor in work efficiency and achieving positive results in life. Support your children in learning how to organize their tasks, set priorities, and make the most of their time. This helps them maintain a work-life balance and achieve significant accomplishments.

5.14 Nurturing Creative Thinking

Creative thinking enables children to generate new solutions and breakthroughs in life. Encourage them to think outside the box, explore new ideas, and constantly learn from new experiences. Creative thinking helps children face complex challenges and make a difference in their work and lives.

5.15 Making Education and Career Choices

Support your children in making decisions about education and choosing careers that align with their passions and abilities. Encourage them to explore and discover areas of interest, so they can choose suitable and exciting paths for their future.

5.16 Learning from Failures and Facing Challenges

In life, no one is exempt from failure and challenges. Teach your children to see failures as valuable lessons and opportunities for growth. Encourage them not to fear failure but to courageously face new challenges. Be their reliable companion and provide encouragement when they need support.

5.17 Building Relationships and Respecting Others

Building relationships and respecting others are crucial factors in helping children form connections and gain support from those around them. Encourage them to learn how to build good relationships with friends, family, and colleagues. Teach them to respect others' opinions and rights and to resolve conflicts peacefully and constructively.

5.18 Creating a Sustainable Future

Lastly, encourage your children to participate in building a sustainable future for themselves and their community. Teach them to respect and care for the environment while engaging in social activities, from charitable work to advocating for the rights of others. By creating a sustainable future, they will contribute to the development and prosperity of the future.

5.19 A Never-Ending Journey

This book is only the beginning of your children's never-ending journey. Remember that life is filled with challenges and new opportunities. Encourage them to continue learning, developing business thinking, and financial management skills, and always innovate and improve themselves.

5.20 Life is an Adventure

Life is an exciting adventure full of surprises. Encourage your children to take risks and explore new things. This adventure will help them grow and become successful in life.

5.22 Taking Action from Advice

The knowledge and advice in this book only hold value when put into action. Encourage your children to apply what they have learned in their daily lives. The essential thing is not just reading and listening, but taking action to truly change and develop.

5.23 Confidence and Patience

Encourage your children to have confidence in their abilities and be patient in achieving their goals. Life may be full of challenges, but with self-belief and perseverance, they will overcome all difficulties.

5.24 Seeking Support and Learning from Others

No one walks alone on the journey of development. Encourage your children to seek support and learn from others. They can find mentors, supportive friends, or experienced individuals in fields of their interest. Learning from others will help them absorb new knowledge and experiences, and broaden their perspectives in life.

5.25 Embracing Change and Adaptation

Life is not linear and is always changing. Encourage your children to be flexible and willing to adjust their plans when necessary. Sometimes, they may have to change directions or adapt to unexpected changes. However, what matters is that they don't give up and continue to walk steadfastly on the path they have chosen.

5.26 Living and Loving

Life is a precious gift, so encourage your children to live fully and cherish every moment. Teach them to appreciate each day and enjoy the small joys in life. Love is the most important thing, so encourage them to treat others well and care for their family, friends, and the community around them.

5.27 Life is Always Welcoming

Life is always open to your children with numerous opportunities and challenges. Encourage them to have an open heart and be willing to embrace new things in life. Every day is an opportunity to learn, grow, and develop.

5.28 Enjoying the Journey

Finally, encourage your children to enjoy every moment of the journey. What matters is not just the destination but the experiences, memories, and lessons they gather along the way. Teach them to savor life and approach the future with a positive and loving attitude.

Chapter 6

Building Financial Mindset
for Your Children

In this chapter, we will continue to focus on building a financial mindset for your children. Financial mindset is the ability to understand and manage money wisely, making sound financial decisions to achieve goals and create a stable future. Let's delve into the essential aspects of financial thinking that your children need to develop.

6.1 Understanding the Value of Money

To build a financial mindset, children need to understand the value of money. Help them realize that money is the result of hard work and time. When they spend a dollar, they have exchanged their effort and time to earn it. It is essential that they do not waste money on things that do not bring true value to their lives.

6.2 Financial Planning

Financial planning is one of the critical skills of financial thinking. Guide your children in creating financial plans based on income, expenses, savings, and investments. With proper planning, they will have a clear view of their financial situation and can make better decisions on how to use their money.

6.3 Saving for a Stable Future

Encourage your children to save money instead of spending it all. Saving is a way to create a stable future with financial backup. Teach them how to build a savings fund to cope with unexpected hardships and also invest in opportunities that can yield benefits.

6.4 Investing for the Future

Help your children understand the benefits and risks of investing. Investing is a way to enhance assets and gain profits in the future. However, they should also be aware of the potential risks and thoroughly research before making investment decisions.

6.5 Smart Debt Management

Debt can be a powerful tool to invest in real estate or business development, but it can also become a burden if not managed properly. Teach your children to manage debt wisely, not borrowing beyond their ability to repay, and maintain a good credit score.

6.6 Persistence with Financial Goals

Financial thinking also demands persistence and direction. Encourage your children to set financial goals and patiently pursue them. Financial thinking is not just about earning money, but also about the ability to maintain and protect assets for the future.

6.7 Early Start is the Key

Finally, encourage your children to start building a financial mindset early on. From simple lessons about saving money to evaluating the value of a product before making a purchase, all contribute to developing a strong financial mindset for the future.

6.8 Practicing Financial Thinking

To truly integrate financial thinking into your children's daily lives, encourage them to practice and apply the knowledge they have learned in real-life situations. Below are some practical activities and lessons that you can use to help your children develop financial thinking:

Lesson 1: Personal Financial Planning Guide your children in creating a personal financial plan by setting short-term, medium-term, and long-term financial goals. They can start by establishing a savings plan for things they want to buy in the future, then move on to setting savings goals for travel, education, or real estate investment.

Lesson 2: Discussing Income and Expenses Engage in discussions with your children about the family's monthly income and expenses. Help them understand the main expenditures, such as shopping expenses, bills, tuition fees, and how your family manages finances to save and invest.

Lesson 3: Managing a Wallet Give your children their own wallet and guide them to manage the money inside it responsibly. Teach them how to record and track daily income and expenses, as it will provide them with a clearer view of their financial situation.

Lesson 4: Evaluating Value Before Purchasing Teach your children how to evaluate the value of a product before making a purchase. They can ask themselves if the product is genuinely necessary and beneficial to their lives. This will help them avoid wasteful spending and save money for more important things.

Lesson 5: Investing in Themselves Encourage your children to invest not only in tangible assets but also in themselves. Encourage them to dedicate time and effort to developing skills, learning from others, and exploring potential career opportunities.

6.9 Support and Encouragement

During the process of developing financial thinking, your children may face difficulties and failures. Be a reliable companion and support them in overcoming challenges. Encourage them to seek new knowledge, learn from mistakes, and not be afraid of failure. Encourage them to seek sources of learning and opportunities to strengthen their financial mindset.

6.10 Celebrating Progress

Finally, celebrate and applaud your children every time they make progress in building their financial mindset. This is a long process that requires patience and determination. Remind them that small daily efforts will lead to significant achievements in the future.

6.11 Conclusion

Chapter 6 has provided knowledge and lessons to help your children build a financial mindset and develop smart money management skills. Be their guide, companion, and support on this journey. Building a financial mindset is a lifelong process and will bring remarkable benefits to your children's lives in the future.

Chapter 7

Mastering Basic Financial Skills

Chapter 7 will focus on mastering essential financial skills that will enable your children to confidently and successfully manage money and achieve their financial goals. Below are some crucial skills that you should teach your children:

7.1 Reading and Understanding Personal Balance Sheets

The personal balance sheet is an essential tool for your children to track their financial situation. Teach them how to read and understand the income, expenses, savings, investments, and debts on the balance sheet. This will help them become familiar with basic financial concepts and manage assets efficiently.

7.2 Creating a Financial Budget

Guide your children in creating a personal financial budget to manage money effectively. Budgeting helps them allocate money to important goals such as daily spending, savings, investments, debt repayment, and entertainment. Encourage them to update and adhere to the budget monthly to maintain stable financial conditions.

7.3 Choosing Suitable Savings Methods

Teach your children about different savings methods and guide them in selecting ones that align with their financial goals. This could include traditional savings in banks, investing in financial products, or contributing to long-term savings funds.

7.4 Building Investment Skills

Investing is a crucial part of developing a financial mindset. Introduce your children to basic investment concepts and help them understand the risks and returns associated with different types of investments. Encourage them to participate in investment activities, such as simulations or real investments with small amounts, to accumulate experience and knowledge.

7.5 Understanding Taxes and Insurance

Taxes and insurance are essential aspects of personal finance. Help your children gain a clear understanding of the types of taxes they need to pay and how to calculate income tax. Additionally, introduce them to important insurance types like health insurance, life insurance, and property insurance to protect assets and cope with unexpected risks.

7.6 Understanding Borrowing and Debt Management

Teach your children about different borrowing methods and how to assess credit before borrowing money. Guide them on rules and strategies for effective debt management to avoid difficulties in debt management. Explain to your children that repaying debts on time and maintaining a good credit score are crucial for achieving financial goals.

7.7 Handling Money Positively in Daily Life

Encourage your children to handle money positively in their daily lives. This includes controlling expenses, avoiding unnecessary spending, and prioritizing important financial goals. Teach them how to take advantage of promotions, discounts, and offers to save money during daily shopping.

7.8 Long-Term Financial Planning

Besides focusing on short-term finances, teach your children about long-term financial planning. Help them shape and pursue larger financial goals such as buying a house, traveling, education, or saving for retirement. Long-term financial planning provides them with a clearer view of the future and direction for financial growth.

7.9 Consideration Before Borrowing or Engaging in Complex Financial Products

Encourage your children to carefully consider before borrowing money or engaging in complex financial products. Sometimes, decisions regarding loans or complex investments can carry high risks. Teach them to research and seek advice from experts before making any money-related decisions.

7.10 Developing Creative Financial Thinking Skills

Lastly, encourage your children to develop creative financial thinking skills. Teach them to seek money-making and investment opportunities creatively. Explore how to connect business and financial knowledge with creativity and discover additional innovative business opportunities.

7.11 Facing the Financial Future with Confidence

Finally, once your children have mastered the basic financial skills and developed a strong financial mindset, they will face their financial future with confidence. Encourage them to value financial awareness and be willing to learn continuously to improve money management skills and achieve success in life.

7.12 Conclusion

Chapter 7 has introduced essential financial skills for your children to master, enabling them to confidently and successfully manage money. From reading personal balance sheets, budgeting, saving, and investing to understanding taxes and debt, these skills will serve as a solid foundation for your children to develop financial thinking and achieve their financial goals.

Continue supporting and accompanying your children in their journey of building a financial mindset and success in life.

Chapter 8

Building Good Financial Habits

Chapter 8 will focus on building good financial habits for your children. Financial habits play a crucial role in maintaining stable financial conditions and achieving financial goals. Below are some steps to help you teach your children to develop positive financial habits:

8.1 Identifying Financial Habits to Develop

Firstly, let's help your children identify the financial habits they need to develop. This may include monthly savings, budget tracking, regular investments, timely debt repayments, and limiting unnecessary expenses. Customize these habits to suit their financial situation and goals.

8.2 Setting Clear and Specific Goals

Assist your children in setting clear and specific financial goals. Goals need to be measurable and have specific time frames. Break down the goals into smaller steps and set schedules to monitor progress. Goal setting helps your children focus and direct their efforts towards what matters most.

8.3 Managing Money Positively

Encourage your children to manage money positively. This includes learning to save, investing wisely, and avoiding unnecessary spending. Remind them of the importance of careful money management to build a stable financial future.

8.4 Practicing Self-Control and Self-Discipline

Teach your children to exercise self-control and self-discipline with their money. This not only involves making financial decisions thoughtfully but also knowing when to resist unnecessary purchases and control spending. Practicing self-control and self-discipline helps your children avoid wasteful spending and live a more financially meaningful life.

8.5 Learning from Experience and Mistakes

No one is perfect, and learning from experience and mistakes is an essential part of building good financial habits. Encourage your children to learn from financial decisions that didn't work out and find ways to improve in the future. Avoid blaming or being overly critical when they make mistakes, but rather encourage them to learn and grow.

8.6 Building Regular Saving Habits

Motivate your children to build regular saving habits. Teach them to set a savings goal and stick to it every month. This helps them accumulate gradually and achieve larger financial goals in the future.

8.7 Addressing Financial Issues Positively

Encourage your children to address financial issues positively. Teach them to seek creative and resourceful ways to handle difficult financial situations. Support and motivate them to face and overcome financial challenges, helping them grow significantly in money management.

8.8 Developing Investment Habits and Growing Assets

Teach your children to develop investment habits and grow their assets. Introduce them to various investment options such as stocks, mutual funds, real estate, and other investment opportunities. Encourage them to research and participate in investment activities to increase their assets and achieve financial sustainability in the future.

8.9 Regularly Evaluating and Adjusting Financial Habits

Lastly, always remind your children that building good financial habits is an ongoing process that requires regular evaluation and adjustments. Encourage them to self-assess their progress and make necessary changes when needed. Nothing is set in stone, and improving financial habits always brings great benefits to their lives.

8.10 Conclusion

Chapter 8 has introduced steps to build positive financial habits for your children. From identifying habits to develop, setting financial goals, managing money, investing, and addressing financial issues, these habits help your children develop financial thinking and achieve success in money management.

Continue supporting and accompanying your children in building positive financial habits and developing a strong financial mindset. Wishing your children success in their journey of building a stable and successful financial future.

Chapter 9

Creating Long-Term Financial Plans

Chapter 9 will focus on creating long-term financial plans for your children. Long-term financial planning helps them shape bigger financial goals and identify specific steps to achieve these goals. Below are the steps to guide your children in creating long-term financial plans:

9.1 Identifying Long-Term Financial Goals

Let's help your children identify their long-term financial goals. This may include buying a house, saving for their children's college education, preparing for retirement, traveling, or investing in their own business. Ensure that these goals are set clearly, specifically, and have specific time frames.

9.2 Evaluating Current Financial Situation

Assist your children in evaluating their current financial situation. This includes examining their income, monthly expenses, assets, debts, and existing investments. Assessing their financial situation will help them identify the starting point and key areas to develop their long-term financial plan.

9.3 Establishing a Roadmap to Achieve Goals

Teach your children to establish a roadmap to achieve their financial goals. Help them create specific steps and timelines to progress towards each sub-goal of the long-term financial plan. Planning to achieve goals will help them easily track progress and ensure they stay on track throughout the process.

9.4 Seeking Financial Opportunities

Encourage your children to seek financial opportunities to support their long-term plan. This includes researching investment programs, learning about effective savings methods, and exploring potential business opportunities. Encourage them to leverage these opportunities to increase their assets and achieve larger financial goals.

9.5 Regularly Assessing and Adjusting the Plan

Remind your children that long-term financial planning is an ongoing process that requires regular assessment and adjustments. Encourage them to monitor progress and make changes as needed. This will help them stay on course and ensure that the long-term financial plan remains aligned with their financial situation and goals.

9.6 Supporting Financial Self-Reliance

Encourage your children to become financially self-reliant. Teach them how to manage money independently and confidently make financial decisions. Support and motivate them when facing financial challenges and encourage continuous learning and development in money management skills.

9.7 Shaping Financial Mindset for the Future

Guide your children in shaping their financial mindset for the future. It's not just about creating a long-term financial plan, but also teaching them to look beyond and consider future financial opportunities and challenges. Encourage them to expand their financial vision and prepare for changes and fluctuations in life.

9.8 Learning from Mentors and Financial Experts

Encourage your children to learn from experienced mentors and financial experts. Inquire about their mistakes and successes in money management. This helps your children gain a better understanding of financial aspects and learn valuable lessons from those who have experienced financial situations before.

9.9 Creating Favorable Conditions for Your Children

Finally, always create favorable conditions for your children to develop their financial mindset and achieve their financial goals. Help them access financial knowledge sources, participate in financial training courses, and provide a supportive environment for their financial development.

9.10 Conclusion

Chapter 9 has addressed creating long-term financial plans for your children. From identifying financial goals, evaluating financial situations, establishing a clear roadmap, seeking financial opportunities, supporting financial self-reliance, shaping financial mindset, learning from mentors and experts, and creating favorable conditions, long-term financial planning helps them build a sustainable and successful financial future.

Continue supporting and accompanying your children in implementing the long-term financial plan and developing a strong financial mindset. Wishing your children success and happiness in their journey of building a stable and successful financial future.

Chapter 10

Creating Sustainable Financial Future

Chapter 10 will focus on creating a sustainable financial future for your children. A sustainable financial future ensures that they have the ability to maintain their lifestyle and achieve financial goals in the long term. Below are the steps to guide your children in creating a sustainable financial future:

10.1 Building an Emergency Fund

Encourage your children to build an emergency fund. This is crucial to ensure that they have enough money to handle unexpected situations such as job loss, significant unforeseen expenses, or medical emergencies. Encourage them to save 3-6 months' worth of living expenses in this emergency fund to protect their personal finances from unexpected risks.

10.2 Adjusting Retirement Plan

Help your children adjust their retirement plan based on their long-term financial goals and current financial situation. Guide them in setting clear retirement goals, determining the amount needed to sustain their lifestyle after retirement, and creating a savings and investment plan to achieve these goals.

10.3 Efficiently Managing Debts

Teach your children to manage debts efficiently. Encourage them to pay debts on time and avoid accumulating excessive debt. Guide them in finding ways to minimize interest on debts and optimize debt repayments. This helps reduce debt burden and ensures financial stability in the future.

10.4 Continued Investing and Asset Growth

Continuously encourage your children to invest and grow their assets. Introduce them to potential investment opportunities and support them in building a diversified and sustainable investment portfolio. Remind them of the importance of long-term investing and patience in capitalizing on asset growth opportunities.

10.5 Property and Life Insurance

Ensure that your children understand the importance of purchasing property and life insurance. Guide them in selecting suitable insurance products to protect their assets and family from unforeseen risks. Insurance plays a vital role in safeguarding personal finances from significant adverse situations.

10.6 Learning and Adapting to Economic Changes

Encourage your children to learn and adapt to economic changes. Teach them to read and understand economic information, research financial market trends, and factors affecting their lives and personal finances. This helps them make informed financial decisions and ensures long-term financial sustainability.

10.7 Regularly Evaluating and Adjusting Finances

Finally, always remind your children that creating a sustainable financial future is an ongoing process. Encourage them to regularly evaluate and adjust their financial plan. This ensures that their financial plan remains aligned with their financial situation and goals throughout different life stages.

10.8 Building a Sustainable Financial Mindset

Encourage your children to build a sustainable financial mindset. This involves understanding the value of money, distinguishing between needs and wants, controlling emotions when making financial decisions, and seeking opportunities to develop financial knowledge through learning and experiences.

10.9 Developing Money Management Skills

Encourage your children to develop money management skills. Teach them how to create a monthly budget, track expenses, save, and invest efficiently. Support them in creating financial plans and prioritizing their financial goals. Money management skills help them build a stable and sustainable financial life.

10.10 Learning from Past Financial Events

Encourage your children to learn from past financial events. Guide them to review both their own and others' mistakes and successes in money management and investment. Learning from previous experiences helps them gain financial control and avoid repeating mistakes.

10.11 Creating a Supportive Environment

Lastly, build a supportive environment for your children's sustainable financial development. Support them in achieving their financial goals and encourage them to believe in their capabilities. A supportive environment helps your children confidently face financial challenges and maintain a positive attitude towards the future.

10.12 Implementing the Financial Plan Together

Encourage your children to implement the financial plan together with their friends or partners. Having a companion in the financial journey can make achieving financial goals easier. Support and motivate each other in the process of saving, investing, and managing money.

10.13 Adaptation and Adjustment in Life

Teach your children to adapt and adjust in life. The financial world is ever-changing and requires flexibility. Encourage them not to fear change and to find ways to adapt to economic and financial changes. Learning how to adjust their financial plans and exploring new methods of money management is essential.

10.14 Continuously Learn and Develop Financially

Encourage your children to continuously learn and develop financially. Finance is a vast field, and there is always something new to learn. Encourage them to participate in courses, training programs, and read books about finance to stay updated with the latest knowledge and enhance their money management skills.

10.15 Stay Focused and Patient

Remind your children to stay focused and patient in pursuing their financial plans. Sometimes, achieving significant and sustainable financial goals may take time and require patience. Encourage them not to give up and to stay determined on their financial journey.

10.16 Regularly Evaluate and Adjust

Finally, remind your children to regularly evaluate and adjust their financial plans. This helps ensure that their financial plans remain aligned with their financial situation and goals. Encourage them to continuously self-assess and improve their financial plans for success and peace of mind regarding their finances.

Chapter 11

Building an Investment Plan

Chapter 11 will focus on building an investment plan for your children. Investment is a crucial part of establishing a sustainable financial future and achieving financial goals in the long run. Here are the steps to guide your children in building a smart investment plan:

11.1 Define Investment Goals

Encourage your children to define their investment goals. This involves identifying specific financial objectives they want to achieve through investing. For example, saving for a home, retirement, or growing wealth.

11.2 Research and Choose Investment Types

Guide your children to research and choose investment types that align with their financial goals. This includes options such as stocks, bonds, mutual funds, financial instruments, and real estate. Explain the risk and return factors for each investment type so that they can make informed decisions.

11.3 Understand Risk and Return

Teach your children to understand the risk and return of each investment type. Clearly explain potential risks associated with investing and how to cope with them. Encourage them to learn fundamental investment principles like risk diversification and optimizing returns.

11.4 Build a Diversified Investment Portfolio

Instruct your children to build a diversified investment portfolio. This involves allocating investment funds into different asset classes to minimize risk and maximize potential profits. Emphasize the importance of maintaining a balanced portfolio over time.

11.5 Define Investment Timeframe

Encourage your children to define their investment timeframe. This includes determining the target investment duration and selecting optimal time periods for investments. Defining the investment timeframe helps them track progress and make adjustments when needed.

11.6 Clarify Investment Strategy

Guide your children in clarifying their investment strategy. This includes deciding whether they want to invest for the long term or short term, automatic or active investing, and selecting investment methods that match their knowledge and experience.

11.7 Monitoring and Evaluating Investment Results

Encourage your children to monitor and evaluate their investment results. Help them understand how to read and analyze investment reports, assess the effectiveness of their investments, and make necessary adjustments when needed.

11.8 Define Investment Costs and Taxes

Guide your children to understand investment costs and taxes associated with the types of assets they invest in. This helps them choose efficient investment options and avoid unnecessary expenses.

11.9 Adjust Investment Plan Based on Financial Situation

Finally, encourage your children to adjust their investment plan according to changes in their financial situation and goals. An investment plan should be flexible and adaptable to new requirements.

11.10 Thoroughly Research Investment Tools

Before investing in any tool, your children should thoroughly research it. They should study the company, product, or project they intend to invest in, read financial reports, and grasp relevant market trends. This helps them make informed investment decisions and consider potential risks.

11.11 Continuously Accumulate Investment Knowledge

Investing is a constantly changing field, so your children need to continuously accumulate knowledge to update their understanding and adjust their investment plans. They can participate in courses, workshops, or learn from financial experts to enhance their knowledge.

11.12 Avoid Emotional Investing

A common mistake in investing is making decisions based on emotions. Your children should avoid investing based on "gut feelings" and instead rely on data and careful evaluation. They should have a specific investment plan and exercise patience to wait for the best investment opportunities.

11.13 Adjust Investment Plan Based on Market Conditions

Financial markets are always changing and can cause fluctuations in your children's investment portfolio. They should regularly review and adjust their investment plan to ensure it aligns with their financial goals and market conditions.

11.14 Seek Professional Advice

If your children feel unsure about investing or want professional guidance, they can seek support from financial experts. An experienced and reputable advisor can help them build an appropriate investment plan and effectively manage their assets.

11.15 Adjust Investment Plan Based on Life Events

Finally, your children should adjust their investment plan based on their life events. Changes in financial situations or personal priorities may require them to modify their initial investment plan.

11.16 Conclusion

Chapter 11 introduced building an investment plan for your children. Investing is a crucial part of establishing a sustainable financial future and achieving financial goals in the long run. From defining investment goals, researching and choosing investment types, understanding risk and return, building a diversified investment portfolio, defining investment timeframe, establishing investment strategy, monitoring and evaluating investment results, defining investment costs and taxes, adjusting investment plan based on financial situation and changing goals, these steps will help your children build a smart and effective investment plan.

Chapter 12

Finance and Family

Chapter 12 will focus on creating a comprehensive financial plan for the family. Managing family finances is an important task that requires cooperation and agreement from all family members. The following are topics to consider when writing this chapter:

12.1 Managing Family Finances

Introduce the significance of managing family finances. Explain that managing family finances is not the responsibility of a single individual but should be carried out through cooperation and agreement from all family members.

12.2 Identifying the Financial Responsibilities of Each Family Member

Guide your children on how to identify the financial responsibilities of each family member. This includes assigning income and expenses to each individual while ensuring that everyone has a role in saving and investing.

12.3 Building a Family Budget

Instruct your children on how to build a family budget. Explain the importance of defining the family's sources of income and expenses, and help them understand how to adjust the budget to meet the family's financial goals and priorities.

12.4 Saving and Investing Together

Encourage your children and the whole family to save and invest together. Explain that working together on saving and investing will help the family achieve common financial goals more quickly and effectively.

12.5 Managing Debts and Repayments

Guide your children on managing debts and repayments within the family. This includes understanding the debt situation and interest rates, creating an effective debt repayment plan, and minimizing unnecessary debts.

12.6 Building a Family Emergency Fund

Encourage your children to build a family emergency fund. This will help the family cope with urgent situations and avoid financial difficulties when unexpected expenses arise.

12.7 Enhancing Financial Knowledge for the Family

Encourage the family to collectively enhance their financial knowledge. This can involve participating in courses, reading financial books and magazines, and dedicating time to discuss family finances to make informed decisions.

12.8 Discussing and Making Collective Financial Decisions

Help your children understand the importance of discussing and making collective financial decisions within the family. This includes open communication, listening, and respecting the opinions of each family member. Consider the following points when discussing and making collective financial decisions:

12.8.1 Planning Family Financial Discussions

Guide your children in planning family financial discussions. Decide on a comfortable time and place where they can engage in discussions without pressure. Encourage them to create a list of topics to be discussed and provide space for each member to share their opinions.

12.8.2 Supporting Family Members in Understanding Finances

Some family members may find it challenging to discuss finances. Encourage your children to support and respect the opinions of these family members. Help them understand basic financial concepts and provide specific information to facilitate effective participation in the discussion.

12.8.3 Consensus on Financial Goals

Encourage your children and the family to set common financial goals. This helps them focus on what matters most and align financial decisions coherently. Emphasize the importance of establishing SMART financial goals (Specific, Measurable, Achievable, Relevant, and Time-bound).

12.8.4 Making Collective Financial Plans

Based on the discussions and opinions of each family member, support your children and the family in making collective financial plans. This may involve choosing investments, setting budgets, or determining saving and investing measures based on common financial goals.

12.9 Supporting and Monitoring Implementation Progress

After the family has made collective financial decisions, support your children in accompanying and monitoring the implementation progress of the financial plan. Help them regularly review and evaluate the family's financial situation and, if necessary, make adjustments to ensure it remains aligned with the financial goals and current circumstances.

12.10 Facing Family and Financial Changes

Guide your children and the family on how to cope with and adapt to these changes. This includes adjusting the financial plan according to changes in income, expenses, and financial goals. Encourage them to be open to seeking support and professional advice if needed to make informed decisions during challenging times.

12.11 Establishing Good Financial Habits in the Family

Financial habits play a crucial role in managing family finances. Encourage your children and the family to develop positive financial habits, such as saving a portion of their income, paying bills on time, and regularly reviewing and evaluating their financial plans. These habits will help the family maintain financial stability and achieve their financial goals.

12.12 Guiding Children on Personal Financial Responsibility

In addition to discussing and managing family finances, it is also important to guide your children on personal financial responsibility. Encourage them to educate themselves and take charge of their personal finances, including managing assets, investing, saving, and debt repayment. Teach them about creating their own financial plans and the significance of making progress in personal finances.

12.13 Continuous Learning and Improving Family Finances

Encourage your children and the family to keep learning and improving their financial knowledge. Teach them how to seek sources of financial literature, books, videos, and materials related to family finances. They can participate in courses or workshops on family finances to stay up-to-date with the latest knowledge and apply it in real-life situations.

12.14 Creating a Positive and Supportive Family Environment

Lastly, encourage your children to create a positive and supportive family environment. This includes fostering joy and harmony in managing finances while supporting and encouraging each other in implementing financial plans and achieving financial goals.

12.15 Conclusion

Chapter 12 has introduced the creation of a general financial plan for the family. Managing family finances is an important task that requires cooperation and consensus from all family members. From managing family finances, identifying financial responsibilities of each member, building budgets, saving and investing together, managing debts and repayments, establishing a family emergency fund, making collective financial decisions, facing family and financial changes, developing good financial habits, guiding personal financial responsibility for children, continuous learning and improving family finances, and creating a positive and supportive family environment, all these steps will help the family achieve financial stability and pave the way for the future.

Chapter 13

Finance and Married Life

Chapter 13 will focus on the role of finance in married life. Managing finances in a marital relationship is an essential aspect that can impact harmony and stability within the family. The following topics should be considered when writing this chapter:

13.1 The Importance of Financial Management in Marriage

Introduce the significance of financial management in a marital relationship. Explain that sensible and effective financial management is a crucial factor in maintaining balance and harmony in married life.

13.2 Building a Joint Financial Plan

Guide how to build a joint financial plan in marriage. This includes identifying common financial goals and specifics for both partners, establishing a family budget, managing money and investments together, and discussing important financial decisions.

13.3 Personal Financial Management in Marriage

In addition to a joint financial plan, encourage your children and their partners to manage their personal finances independently. Explain that having individual accounts will help maintain financial independence and ensure privacy in managing money.

13.4 Handling Financial Conflicts in Marriage

Guide how to handle financial conflicts in marriage. Encourage your children and their partners to be honest in discussing finances, listen to and respect each other's perspectives, and find ways to resolve conflicts harmoniously and effectively.

13.5 Setting Financial Goals Together

Encourage your children and their partners to jointly determine financial goals. Assist them in discussing and making decisions about saving and investing to achieve these goals together. Share the joy and achievements when reaching shared financial goals.

13.6 Resolving Financial Issues in Marriage

Guide on how to resolve financial issues in marriage. If there are conflicts or disagreements about finances, encourage your children and their partners to have honest and open discussions. Work together to find solutions and prioritize the family's common interests.

13.7 Respecting Each Other's Financial Decisions

Help your children and their partners respect each other's financial decisions. Whether it's shared financial management or independent management, emphasize equality and freedom in making financial choices.

13.8 Conclusion

Chapter 13 has introduced the role of finance in married life. Managing finances in marriage requires cooperation, honesty, and consensus from both sides. From building a joint financial plan, managing personal finances, handling financial conflicts, setting financial goals together, and respecting each other's financial decisions, all these steps will help married life become harmonious and stable in financial management and build a better financial future for the family.

Chapter 14

Investment and Building Assets

Chapter 14 will focus on investment and building assets. Investment is a crucial part of managing personal and family finances, helping to increase assets and achieve financial goals. The following topics should be considered when writing this chapter:

14.1 The Importance of Investment

Introduce the significance of investment in building assets and achieving financial goals. Explain that investment can help increase the value of assets over time and generate profits.

14.2 Understanding Investment Options

Guide your children to understand various investment options. Explain common investment assets such as stocks, bonds, mutual funds, real estate, and cryptocurrencies. Present the benefits and risks of each type of investment to help them make informed decisions.

14.3 Defining Investment Goals

Encourage your children to identify specific investment goals. Ask them whether they want to invest for capital preservation, asset growth, retirement savings, or other financial objectives. This will help them select investments that align with their goals.

14.4 Assessing Personal Financial Situation before Investing

Before investing, encourage your children to assess their personal financial situation. Ensure they have sufficient emergency funds, manageable debt levels, and the ability to bear risks associated with investments. If necessary, encourage them to seek professional financial advice for a comprehensive understanding of their financial situation.

14.5 Choosing an Investment Strategy

Guide how to choose an investment strategy that suits their goals and personal financial situation. This includes determining their risk tolerance, investment time horizon, and allocation of different types of investments in their investment portfolio.

14.6 Understanding Real Estate Investment

Encourage your children to learn about real estate investment. This includes understanding the real estate market, identifying potential investment opportunities, and effectively managing real estate assets.

14.7 Understanding Bond and Mutual Fund Investments

Guide your children to understand bond and mutual fund investments. Explain the mechanics of bonds and mutual funds and how to select and monitor the performance of mutual funds effectively.

14.8 Investing and Key Considerations

Below are some key considerations when investing:

• Investing does not guarantee high returns and always comes with risks. Encourage your children to invest based on specific financial goals and be prepared for the possibility of losses.

• Encourage your children to diversify their investments. This helps to minimize risks and increase growth opportunities.

• Always listen to and seek advice from reliable financial experts before investing in any type of asset. Understanding the risks and benefits of different investments will help them make informed decisions.

• Understanding and monitoring the financial market is crucial for investment. Encourage your children to spend time researching and understanding market fluctuations and economic conditions to make accurate investment decisions.

• Investment is a long-term process, so encourage your children not to worry too much about short-term market fluctuations. Emphasize that patience and maintaining the investment strategy are important for achieving better results in the future.

• Encourage your children to focus their investments on long-term goals, such as retirement savings or their children's education. This will help them stay focused on progress and achieving important life goals.

14.9 Building Assets Together

Investment and building assets are processes that your children and their partners can engage in together. Encourage them to accompany and support each other in achieving financial goals and building sustainable assets.

14.10 Investment Management and Profit Optimization

Guide your children on how to manage investments intelligently. They should regularly monitor and evaluate the effectiveness of their investments, making adjustments if necessary to optimize profits and minimize risks.

14.11 Risk Mitigation in Investment

Investment always comes with risks, but encourage your children to minimize risks by diversifying their investments and avoiding overly risky assets. Encourage them to learn about tools and techniques for risk mitigation in investments.

14.12 Conclusion

Chapter 14 has introduced investment and building assets. Investment is a crucial part of managing personal and family finances, helping to increase assets and achieve financial goals. From understanding investment options, defining investment goals, assessing the financial situation before investing, choosing an investment strategy, learning about real estate and mutual fund investments, to key considerations when investing and risk mitigation, all these steps will help your children build and develop sustainable assets in the future.

Chapter 15

Finance and Retirement

Chapter 15 will focus on finance and asset management as one enters retirement. Retirement is an important stage in life when your children transition from working to retirement. Managing finances properly and building a financial plan to prepare for retirement is essential. The following topics should be considered when writing this chapter:

15.1 Financial Preparation for Retirement

Introduce the importance of financial preparation for retirement. Encourage your children to understand the necessity of saving and investing to have a stable and comfortable financial future after retirement.

15.2 Determining the Financial Amount Needed for Retirement

Guide how to determine the financial amount needed to maintain a comfortable lifestyle during retirement. Encourage your children to consider expected expenses after retirement, including daily living expenses, healthcare costs, and retirement funds, to calculate the minimum amount they need to save and invest.

15.3 Understanding Retirement Savings Options

Introduce various retirement savings options, including high-interest savings, government retirement plans, and employer-sponsored retirement funds. Help your children understand and choose options that suit their financial situation and retirement goals.

15.4 Understanding Retirement Funds and Healthcare Insurance Plans

Guide your children to understand retirement funds and healthcare insurance plans after retirement. This includes learning about retirement accounts like IRA and 401(k) and government healthcare and retirement plans.

15.5 Building a Financial Plan for Retirement

Encourage your children to build a detailed financial plan for retirement. This involves identifying retirement goals, calculating the amount needed to achieve those goals, and choosing appropriate savings and investment tools to execute the plan.

15.6 Financial Support in Retirement

Encourage your children to research and understand available sources of financial support during retirement. This includes learning about government programs such as Medicare and Medicaid, as well as various types of financial assistance from nonprofit organizations and local governments.

15.7 Choosing a Financial Plan After Retirement

Assist your children in selecting a suitable financial plan for retirement. Encourage them to consider options such as continuing investments, setting up an emergency fund, planning for relocation, and exploring part-time work to maintain a happy and fulfilling life after retirement.

15.8 Conclusion

Chapter 15 has introduced finance and asset management as one enters retirement. Managing finances wisely and building a financial plan for retirement is crucial to ensuring a comfortable and stable life after retirement. From financial preparation for retirement, determining the required financial amount, understanding retirement savings options, grasping retirement funds and healthcare insurance plans, building a financial plan for retirement, seeking financial support during retirement, to choosing a financial plan after retirement, all these steps will help your children lead a solid and peaceful life after retirement.

Chapter 16

Debt Management and

Financial Empowerment

Chapter 16 will focus on debt management and financial empowerment. Debt can be a significant challenge in managing personal and family finances, but with a proper plan and strategy, your children can reduce debt and achieve financial stability. The following topics should be considered when writing this chapter:

16.1 The Importance of Debt Management

Introduce the importance of debt management. Emphasize that debt can create financial stress and limit investment and savings opportunities. Encourage your children to approach debt responsibly and carefully evaluate their ability to repay debts.

16.2 Identifying and Estimating Debt

Guide your children in identifying and estimating their total debt. Encourage them to list all debts, including credit card debt, loans, student loans, and others. This will provide them with an overview of their debt situation.

16.3 Reviewing Debts and Calculating Interest Rates

Assist your children in reviewing their debts and calculating interest rates. They should examine the borrowing terms and interest rates of each debt and also consider credit card policies and loan conditions.

16.4 Creating a Detailed Debt Repayment Plan

Encourage your children to create a detailed debt repayment plan. This includes determining the amount they can allocate monthly for debt repayment, prioritizing higher-interest debts for early repayment, and establishing a specific repayment schedule to keep the process organized.

16.5 Learning to Adjust Spending Habits

Motivate your children to adjust their spending habits to reduce debt. This involves limiting credit card usage, cutting unnecessary expenses, and establishing a reasonable budget to control their spending.

16.6 Financial Empowerment and Building an Emergency Fund

Guide your children in financial empowerment and building an emergency fund to deal with financial difficulties and reduce future debt. They should learn effective ways to save and invest, as well as consider creating an emergency fund to be prepared for unexpected situations.

16.7 Conclusion

Chapter 16 has introduced debt management and financial empowerment. Debt management is a critical factor in achieving financial sustainability and ensuring a stable financial life. From identifying and estimating debt, reviewing debts and calculating interest rates, creating a detailed debt repayment plan, adjusting spending habits, financial empowerment, and building an emergency fund, all these steps will help your children minimize debt and achieve financial stability.

Chapter 17

Financial Risk Management

Chapter 17 will focus on financial risk management in life. Financial risks cannot be completely avoided, but your children can learn to face and minimize them to protect their personal and family finances. The following topics should be considered when writing this chapter:

17.1 Understanding Financial Risk

Introduce the concept of financial risk and the importance of understanding and facing risks. Encourage your children to be aware of common financial risks such as market risk, job risk, health risk, and natural risk.

17.2 Identifying Personal Risks

Guide your children in identifying personal risks they may face in life. They should consider factors such as job loss, income reduction, unexpected healthcare costs, and other emergency situations that may impact their finances.

17.3 Evaluating Financial Risk

Encourage your children to assess the level of risk and their ability to withstand risks. They should consider their current financial situation, the level of emergency savings, and their financial capacity to determine what level of risk is reasonable for them.

17.4 Strategies for Risk Mitigation

Assist your children in developing strategies to mitigate financial risks. This includes building an emergency fund, obtaining suitable insurance coverage (such as health insurance, car insurance, and home insurance), diversifying investments, and implementing safety measures in investment decisions.

17.5 Learning to Handle Financial Emergencies

Encourage your children to learn how to handle financial emergencies. This involves identifying emergency measures, such as cutting expenses, seeking additional employment, or finding alternative income sources if necessary.

17.6 Conclusion

Chapter 17 has introduced financial risk management. Financial risks cannot be completely avoided, but your children can learn to face and minimize them to protect their personal and family finances. From understanding financial risks, identifying personal risks, evaluating financial risks, implementing risk mitigation strategies, learning to handle financial emergencies, all these steps will help your children build a strong and secure financial foundation.

Chapter 18

Finance and Family

Chapter 18 will focus on finance and asset management within the family. Managing family finances is a complex process that requires cooperation and understanding among family members. The following topics should be considered when writing this chapter:

18.1 Family Financial Management: Importance

Introduce the importance of family financial management. Encourage your children to recognize the significance of cooperation and communication within the family to achieve common financial goals and build a solid financial foundation.

18.2 Creating a Family Budget

Guide your children in creating a family budget. They should work together to assess the family's income and expenses, identify common financial goals, and allocate responsibilities in managing family finances.

18.3 Establishing a Family Emergency Fund

Encourage your children to establish a family emergency fund to deal with unforeseen circumstances and minimize financial risks. This includes determining the required amount for unexpected expenses and building a suitable emergency fund.

18.4 Financial Aspects of Marriage

Assist your children in facing financial challenges in marriage. They should collaborate to assess each other's financial situations and discuss long-term financial plans for the marriage, including asset management, sharing responsibilities, and setting long-term financial goals.

18.5 Managing Children's Finances

Introduce the concept of managing children's finances. Encourage your children to teach their children about money, saving, and investing from an early age to help them understand finance and develop positive financial habits.

18.6 Financial Guidance for Seniors

Guide your children in helping the seniors in the family with financial management and financial planning. This includes assisting them with financial procedures, evaluating their financial situation, and ensuring they have enough finances to live comfortably.

18.7 Conclusion

Chapter 18 has introduced family finances and asset management. Managing family finances is a complex process that requires cooperation and understanding among family members. From building a family budget, creating emergency funds, managing financial matters in marriage, handling finances for children, to providing financial guidance for seniors, all of these aspects play crucial roles in achieving financial stability and security within the family.

Conclusion

Financial Journey with Your Children

We have embarked on a wonderful financial journey with your children. This book was written with the intention of imparting knowledge and experience to help them build a strong financial foundation and face the future with confidence. Throughout the writing process, we have learned about the importance of understanding personal finance, budget management, investing and saving, building emergency funds, minimizing financial risks, family finances, and financial management during important life events.

Teaching children financial management is not only about imparting knowledge about money but also a process of interaction and learning together. We have seen positive changes in your children as they gained knowledge about money, learned how to manage income, set financial goals, and build a prosperous future.

Remember that financial management is not an arduous task. With the support, guidance, and care of parents, your children can become wise and confident financial managers. Encourage them to continue learning, honing financial skills, and applying the knowledge from this book in their daily lives.

This book does not end here. The financial journey with your children continues. Keep learning, face challenges, and seize opportunities to grow stronger in life. By journeying together, we can create positive changes and build a promising financial future.

Finally, I want to express sincere gratitude to the readers for taking the time to read this book. I hope that the content of the book has provided support and value in teaching children financial management. May this book become a useful and reliable resource on your children's financial journey.

Let's together build a strong and promising financial future for your children!

Sincerely,

www.ingramcontent.com/pod-product-compliance
Lightning Source LLC
Chambersburg PA
CBHW062239290526
45794CB00006B/2344